A HOME IN THE BIOME

At Home in the

MOUNTAINS

Louise and Richard Spilsbury

PowerKiDS press™

New York

Published in 2016 by **The Rosen Publishing Group**
29 East 21st Street, New York, NY 10010

Produced for Rosen by Calcium
Editors: Sarah Eason and Amanda Learmonth
Designers: Paul Myerscough and Emma DeBanks

Picture credits: Cover: Shutterstock: Xseon; Insides: Dreamstime: Alain 12–13,
Dhprophotog 12, Dennis Donohue 17, Erwin F. 19, Jiri Kulhanek 7, Svyatoslav
Lypynskyy 10–11, Marcoinno 21, Martinased 11, Pstedrak 6–7, Tavitopai 8–9,
Michael Woodruff 9, Minyun Zhou 4–5, 29; Shutterstock: bjul 22–23, canadastock
14–15, Sorin Colac 27, Sam DCruz 18–19, Dennis W. Donohue 23, Erick Margarita
Images 28–29, Brian Lasenby 5, pchais 24–25, Mike Peters 16–17, Josh Schutz
25, Tim Stirling 26–27, Tadeas 1, 15, Camelia Varsescu 20–21.

Cataloging-in-Publication Data
Spilsbury, Louise.
At home in the mountains / by Louise and Richard Spilsbury.
p. cm. — (A home in the biome)
Includes index.
ISBN 978-1-5081-4563-9 (pbk.)
ISBN 978-1-5081-4564-6 (6-pack)
ISBN 978-1-5081-4565-3 (library binding)
1. Mountains — Juvenile literature. I. Spilsbury, Louise.
II. Spilsbury, Richard, 1963-. III. Title.
GB512.S75 2016
551.43'2—d23

Manufactured in the United States of America
CPSIA Compliance Information: Batch BW16PK: For Further Information contact Rosen Publishing, New York, New York at 1-800-237-9932

Contents

At Home up High

Mountains are one of the most challenging biomes in the world. At lower levels, there are grassy slopes and forests, but it gets colder and windier as you climb higher. The tops of the world's tallest mountains are often cloaked in heavy clouds, blasted by strong winds, and covered in ice and snow. The amazing plants and animals that survive there have adapted to live in these harsh conditions.

Suited to the Mountains

Bighorn sheep are adapted for climbing over rough, rocky mountain slopes. Their hooves are divided into two to help the sheep keep their balance. The hooves have rough bottoms that grip the rocks. Bighorn sheep have excellent eyesight so they can move around quickly and easily.

*Bighorn sheep calves are safer from **predators** on high mountain ledges.*

HOME SWEET HOME

Bighorn sheep move up and down the mountains. In the winter, they climb down to feed on seeds and plants while the high mountains are covered in snow. When it warms up in the spring, they climb high to have their babies on rocky ledges, safe from predators.

Edelweiss

When we are somewhere cold and windy, we drop our heads and hold our arms close to our bodies to keep warm. Some plants use a similar tactic to survive the chilly temperatures high up in the mountaintops.

Lying Low

Edelweiss is a pretty wildflower that grows in clumps just 3 inches to 8 inches (8 to 20 cm) above the ground. By growing in low mats like this, the plant keeps out of the path of the strongest winds. The short stems of the edelweiss grow close together to help it trap heat between the stems.

Edelweiss plants grow long roots into rock cracks. The roots anchor the plants to the mountain. The roots also reach pockets of water below the rocks when water near the surface is frozen into ice.

HOME SWEET HOME

Edelweiss leaves are covered in a layer of fine, fuzzy hairs. It can be very cold high up in the mountains, but the sun also burns strongly there. The fine hairs on the leaves protect the plant from rays of sunlight that could burn and harm it, and they keep the plant warm, too.

The silvery-white color of edelweiss leaves and their fine hairs help them reflect strong sunlight that might harm the tiny yellow flowers in the plant's center.

Spruce Trees

It can get very cold and windy high up on a mountain, so only the strongest trees can live there. Mighty spruce trees are tough enough to survive heavy snows and being blasted by strong, icy winds.

Surviving Snow and Ice

Spruce trees are **conifer** trees. Conifer trees have narrow, waxy leaves that look like needles. Trees with broad, flat leaves, such as oak trees, have to drop their leaves in the winter to keep them from being damaged by snow and ice. Conifer leaves are tough and their narrow shape keeps ice from collecting on them, so conifer trees can keep their green leaves all year round. That is why these trees are often called evergreens.

Spruce trees are tall, and some can grow up to 330 feet (100 m) high. They have strong trunks, but their branches are surprisingly flexible. This is useful in the winter. The spruce trees' branches bend under the weight of snow, and it then slides off them.

Mountain chickadees pluck insects and seeds from spruce trees.

HOME SWEET HOME

A plant's flowers can be destroyed by cold, so spruce trees grow their seeds in **cones**. Cones are made up of a lot of hard, overlapping **scales**. Tucked in between the scales, the seeds grow safely.

Mountain Pine Beetles

Mountain pine beetles have a special way of surviving the cold, harsh mountain weather. They only live for about a year and they spend most of their short life under the protective bark of pine trees.

Babies to Adults

In the summer, adult pine beetles leave the pine trees in which they were born. They fly to a new tree and start burrowing through the bark of the tree. They make long tunnels called galleries under the bark, then lay their eggs in them. The small, maggot-like **larvae** hatch out of the eggs, crawl under the bark, and feed on sugars that the tree makes to feed itself. In the spring, the larvae develop into adults and then they fly off to lay eggs in new pine trees.

Pine beetles burrow under bark to keep warm. They also make sugars in their blood that keep them from freezing up, a little like the **antifreeze** people put into cars in winter!

HOME SWEET HOME

When beetles make holes in bark, sticky **resin** oozes out to trap and kill them. That is why a lot of beetles attack one tree at the same time. Some are caught in the resin, but many survive. As more and more beetles dig into the bark, the resin ooze slows down.

Snowshoe Hares

When you look at snowshoe hares you can see how these mountain animals got their name! Their big, furry feet act like snowshoes to keep them from sinking into the snow. In fact, snowshoe hares have extremely thick fur all over their bodies. This keeps them warm when they scurry about in search of grass and other food to eat.

Changing Color

The other amazing thing about snowshoe hares is that they can change color. In the winter, they have coats of white fur. This helps them blend in with the snow and hides them from coyotes, eagles, and other animals that hunt them. When the snow melts each spring, their white winter fur falls out and is replaced by brown fur. This helps them blend in with the mountain rocks that are revealed after the snow melts.

*In the spring and summer, a snowshoe hare's fur turns brown to help **camouflage** it against the mountain rocks.*

The snowshoe hare's big feet help it jump and run quickly over mountains. A snowshoe hare can travel at speeds of almost 30 miles per hour (48 kph) and leap 10 feet (3 m) in a single bound. It can also change direction suddenly and jump straight into the air to escape predators.

Marmots

Marmots are cute, chubby little mammals that have several adaptations to help them survive high up in a mountain biome.

Snuggling up for the Winter

Marmot burrows have long tunnels that lead to a big room called a den. This is where families sleep together during the winter months. Marmots use their strong claws to dig burrows in hard and even frozen ground. All year round they can escape into these burrows and huddle together to keep warm when it is cold and windy outside.

In the fall, marmots go into their burrow and seal off the entrance with hay and grass. It is time to **hibernate**! They cuddle close together and go into a deep sleep. Their breathing and heart rate slows down, and they stay inside the burrow until the worst of the winter is over.

Marmots are greedy animals. They spend all spring and summer eating leaves and flowers to get as fat as they can. This helps them survive the cold winters while they hibernate, and when their food dies back or is covered in snow.

Marmots have a thick layer of fat and fur to keep them warm and cozy. They have sharp claws, strong shoulder and leg muscles for digging tunnels, and large teeth for chewing and gnawing.

15

Mountain Lions

Mountain lions, or pumas, are the top mountain predators. They travel far and wide in search of animals such as mice, deer, and moose to eat. To survive, they have to be able to move quickly over rugged mountain slopes.

Jump, Run, Swim!

Mountain lions have unusually long back legs, huge paws, and very long tails. Their long, strong legs and big feet help them jump and run quickly, and their long tails help them balance when they jump high or far. They can even swim through mountain rivers if they need to chase down **prey**. Mountain lions have excellent eyesight and hearing to help them find prey.

A mountain lion can jump 20 feet (6 m) up a cliff and leap 40 feet (12 m) downhill! Its long claws also help it climb trees to escape bigger predators, such as jaguars and bears.

HOME SWEET HOME

A mountain lion hunts by hiding behind grass, bushes, and rocks and sneaking up on its prey. Only when it gets very close to its prey does it rush out and attack. When it rests, it finds shelter in mountain caves, rocks, bushes, or clumps of trees.

Mountain Gorillas

Mountain gorillas are the biggest gorillas in the world. They live among the trees in mountain forests. It is often cloudy and damp in these forests and it gets very cold at night.

Hungry Gorillas

Mountain gorillas have long, thick black hair that helps keep their large bodies warm when the temperature drops below freezing. They feed on leaves, shoots, and stems of mountain plants. These plants can be tough, but mountain gorillas rip the plants easily with their huge, strong hands and bite through them with their super-sharp teeth. Mountain gorillas spend a lot of their time eating and relaxing, because it takes a long time to **digest** their leafy meals.

Mountain gorillas can walk upright on two legs, but they usually move around the mountains on all fours.

HOME SWEET HOME

Mountain gorillas can climb trees but they spend most of the day on the ground. At night, they make a nest in the trees or on the ground. They break and bend branches and leaves to wrap around themselves for warmth.

Thick, dark hair helps keep mountain gorillas warm. Young gorillas cuddle up to their mothers in their nests for warmth.

Condors

Condors soar above mountains, flying easily above the rocky, dangerous land. They are on the lookout for dead animals below. As soon as they spot one, they swoop down to feed.

Long-distance Flier

Condors' long wings make them expert fliers. They usually fly at speeds of about 30 miles per hour (48 kph) and travel around 50 miles (80 km) a day in search of food. The condor's beak is large and sharp. It is strong enough to tear open the tough skin of horses and cattle, and break the bones of animals such as goats and pigs.

When a condor eats, it often sticks its whole head into the body of a dead animal. Dead and rotting animals are full of harmful **bacteria**. Having a bald head keeps bacteria and rotting flesh from sticking to the condor's head and making it sick.

The condor's large wings help it fly upward on mountain breezes.

HOME SWEET HOME

Condors make nests of sticks and twigs high up on rocky mountain ledges. Their chicks, which cannot fly until they are six months old, are safe from predators there. The chicks' parents bring them food and care for them until they are ready to leave the nest.

Elks

Elks are very big red deer that live in mountain biomes. The males have huge antlers on their heads that may reach 4 feet (1.2 m) tall. They use these antlers for fighting.

Summer and Winter

Elks cope with the challenges of living on a mountain by **migrating**. In the early summer, they travel to feeding grounds high up on the mountain. There the females have their babies, which can stand just 20 minutes after being born!

In the winter, when plants high up the mountain are buried deep under snow, elks gather together into large herds and return to feeding grounds lower down the mountain. During the winter months, elks grow a long, thick coat of hair to keep them warm. In the spring, this hair falls out and they grow a new coat of shorter, cooler hair for the summer. In the fall, the short coat falls out and long, winter hair grows once again.

HOME SWEET HOME

Deep snow can be difficult to walk through. Elks have wide hooves that help them walk long distances, climb steep surfaces, and walk over snow rather than sinking down into it.

Elks spend the winter eating shrubs that poke out above the layer of snow, or clearing patches of snow with their hooves to eat the grass below.

Mountain Goats

Mountain goats are the world's most impressive climbers. They scramble up and down rocky mountain slopes at high speeds and rarely slip or stumble. They are so well-adapted to mountain life that they are the largest mammals found in high mountain regions.

Super Hoofers!

The secret to mountain goats' success is their hooves. These are wide and split into two halves that can spread to grip a large rock surface. The hooves also have rubbery pads on the bottom that provide grip and help the goats jump from rock to rock. Mountain goats also have special extra claws at the back of their hooves that keep them from slipping when they run downhill, and allow them to safely climb down incredibly steep slopes.

Mountain goats and their young can climb quickly up slippery slopes and rocks to escape predators.

HOME SWEET HOME

In the winter, mountain goats grow long beards and two layers of white fur. This protects them from icy temperatures and freezing winds. It also provides them with camouflage against the snow. Their white coat blends in with the snow while they munch on grasses, mosses, and other mountain plants. This makes it harder for predators to spot the goats.

Black Bears

Black bears are covered in many layers of shaggy fur, which helps keep them warm. To escape the worst of the winter weather and survive on high mountains, black bears hibernate in cozy dens.

Summer Feasts, Winter Sleeps

During the summer, black bears eat as much as they can and most double their weight by the fall. In the fall, they make dens in caves, burrows, piles of branches, or other places that are sheltered and out of sight. When the winter comes, the bears go to sleep in their dens and live off the body fat they built up in the summer and fall.

Female black bears give birth to their cubs during hibernation. They feed the cubs on milk from their bodies until the spring, when the mothers and their babies leave their dens in search of food.

Black bears survive in mountain biomes because they are **omnivores**. They eat both plants and meat. They eat roots, berries, grass, and other plants but also fish, insects, and animals such as deer. When one type of food is scarce on a mountain, they simply eat another.

Black bears catch fish from mountain streams and rivers. Their long noses give them an incredible sense of smell. Their noses also help them find food and avoid danger.

Mountains Under Threat

Mountains are important biomes for some awesome plants and animals. Yet people are damaging or destroying some of these mountain homes. People cut down mountain forests to use the wood or to clear the land to make space for mines or farms. This means there are fewer trees to provide animals with food and shelter.

Protecting Our Mountains

Around the world, people are trying to protect mountain biomes. They study mountains to see how changes affect plants and animals. They tell people about the importance of protecting mountains and they plant trees to restore mountain forests. **Conservation** groups also raise money to help protect **endangered** mountain animals such as the giant panda.

Giant panda numbers are increasing. In 2014, a survey counted 1,864 pandas. That was 16 percent more than the previous count in 2004.

HOME SWEET HOME

Giant pandas eat only certain types of bamboo plants that grow on the mountains of China. They need to eat a lot of bamboo every day. When people cut down bamboo plants, fewer plants remain for the pandas to eat. In some places, people are making reserves for pandas. These are areas of land that are protected and where giant pandas can live safely.

Glossary

adapted Changed to survive in an environment.

antifreeze A substance that keeps engine liquids from freezing in a car.

bacteria Tiny living things too small to see. Bacteria can cause disease.

bark The tough outer layer around the trunk of a tree.

biomes Communities of plants and animals living together in a certain kind of climate.

camouflage A color or pattern that matches the surrounding environment and helps an organism hide.

cones Parts produced by conifer trees to contain their seeds.

conifer A type of tree that has needle-like leaves and produces its seeds in cones.

conservation The act of guarding, protecting, or preserving something.

digest To break down food so it can be absorbed by the body.

endangered When a plant or animal is in danger of dying out.

hibernate To go into a special long sleep to survive cold winters when there is little food to eat.

larvae Animals at the stage when they have just hatched out of eggs.

mammals Types of animals that feed their babies with milk from their bodies.

migrating Moving from one place to another in different seasons.

omnivores Animals that eat plants and other animals.

predators Animals that catch and eat other animals.

prey An animal that is caught and eaten by other animals.

resin A thick, sticky substance made by trees to seal holes in their bark.

scales Small, overlapping plates of hard material.

Further Reading

Bow, James. *Mountains Inside Out* (Ecosystems Inside Out). New York, NY: Crabtree Publishing Company, 2015.

Ganeri, Anita. *Exploring Mountains: A Benjamin Blog and His Inquisitive Dog Investigation* (Exploring Habitats with Benjamin Blog and His Inquisitive Dog). Mankato, MN: Heinemann-Raintree, 2015.

Hinman, Bonnie. *Keystone Species that Live in the Mountains* (Kid's Guide to Keystone Species in Nature). Hockessin, DE: Mitchell Lane Publishers, Inc., 2015.

Hirsch, Rebecca E. *Mountain Gorillas: Powerful Forest Mammals* (Comparing Animal Traits). Minneapolis, MN: Lerner Publishing Group, 2015.

Royston, Angela. *Mountain Food Chains* (Young Explorer: Food Chains and Webs). Mankato, MN: Heinemann-Raintree, 2015.

Websites

PowerKids Press has developed an online list of websites related to the subject of this book. This site is updated regularly. Please use this link to access the list: **www.powerkidslinks.com/ahitb/mountains**

Index